D1631229

# Chimney Charlie

Stories linking with the History
National Curriculum Key Stage 2.

ROTHERHAM LIBRARY &
INFOR        SERVICES

JF
B4804712146
L/03525
SCHOOLS STOCK

First published in 1999 by Franklin Watts
96 Leonard Street, London EC2A 4XD

Text © Roy Apps 1999

The right of Roy Apps to be identified as
the Author of this Work has been asserted by
him in accordance with the Copyright, Designs
and Patents Act, 1988

**Editor:** Lesley Bilton
**Designer:** Jason Anscomb
**Consultant:** Dr Anne Millard, BA Hons, Dip Ed, PhD

A CIP catalogue record for this book
is available from the British Library.

ISBN 0 7496 3351 4 (hbk)
     0 7496 3551 7 (pbk)

Dewey Classification 941.081

Printed in Great Britain

# Chimney Charlie

by **Roy Apps**

**Illustrations by Julie Anderson**

**FRANKLIN WATTS**
NEW YORK•LONDON•SYDNEY

# 1

## A Hard Day's Work

Charlie Thompsett shivered. The room was cold, for no fire had been lit in the hearth that morning.

"Take yer coat off, boy!" commanded Scroat. "And yer boots!"

Jeremiah Scroat was a Master Sweep.

Charlie was his climbing boy and this was his first job.

Scroat began fixing a cloth across the

hearth. "Should be easy enough this one, even for a new 'un like yourself," he said, curling his lip in a leer. "About 35 feet tall and 15 by 10 inches wide, I reckon."

Charlie shivered again. Not just from cold, but from fear.

"Get behind the cloth," Scroat hissed. "Come on, boy! We ain't got all day. There's another six chimneys to do before the morning's out!"

Charlie stepped behind the cloth. It
was pitch black. Through
the material he could
make out
Scroat's shadow.
As the cloth
moved he saw it
fluttering like a
black, evil ghost.
Suddenly the
ghost was gone
and Scroat was
standing at his
side.

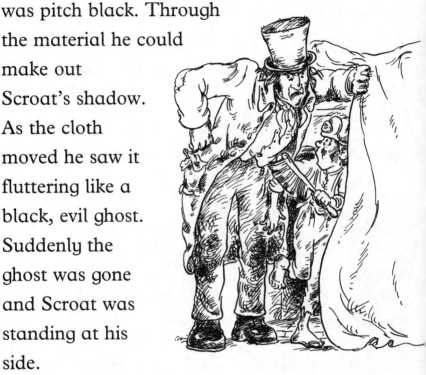

"Up!" he snarled.

Charlie pushed his brush up the
chimney. Too late, he remembered that he
was supposed to pull his sweep's cap down
over his face. His brush dislodged a pocket

of soot which dropped straight into his eyes, making them sting. But before he had time to wipe them, Charlie felt a pair of rough hands grab his ankles and lift him right off the ground.

"Go on! Like I showed yer! Push with your elbows and knees. Push!"

Numb now with fear, Charlie pulled his sweep's cap over his face and forced himself up. Holding his brush above his head with one hand, he pushed against the sides of the chimney with his body.

Slowly Charlie inched his way up the inside of the tall chimney like a human caterpillar. As he swept the soot fell over him on its way down to the hearth below. It was so dark he found it hard to tell if his eyes were open or shut. It was silent too, except for the tap-tap of his brush as it searched out the path of the chimney above him.

Eventually Charlie felt a sudden blast of cold about his ears. He was near the top. With one final push his head

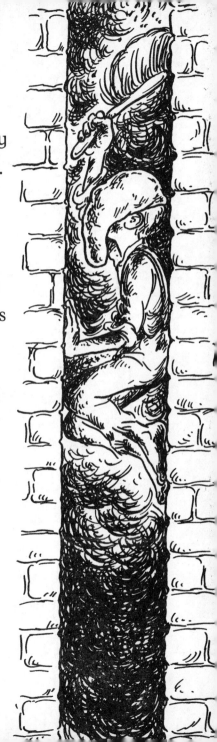

cleared the chimney stack and he found
himself peering out across the frosty, early
morning roof tops of the town.

"What are you doing up there, boy?" A
voice echoed faintly but harshly up the
chimney below him.

Charlie pressed his knees in and began to slide back down the chimney. He pushed himself down the small bend faster than he should have done. The rough chimney bricks ripped at his shirt and trousers and then at his elbows and knees. He landed in a sooty heap at Scroat's feet, his elbows and knees bloody and stinging with pain.

While the housekeeper paid Scroat, Charlie put on his jacket. He looked around for his boots and with alarm saw Scroat giving them to the housekeeper – for money! Scroat caught his look.

"You'll not be needing these, boy," he said to Charlie. "You can walk barefoot. It'll save you having to take 'em off and put 'em back on each time we get a job." He laughed coarsely.

Outside most of the rest of the world was still not awake. Scroat set off. Charlie, barefoot now and laden with his bag of soot, trotted after him.

"Sw–e–e–p!" called Scroat as they walked along. "Sw–e–e–p!"

Sometimes a maid or housekeeper would call them in, and then up another chimney Charlie would climb. By the time they had finished he could hardly bear to touch his knees and elbows, let alone press them against the rough chimney bricks.

Charlie followed Scroat towards his lodging. The sack of soot on his back weighed heavy from half a dozen chimneys. The smells drifting from the various hot pie stalls teased Charlie's nostrils. He was hungry.

"Jes' you wait here for me, boy," growled Scroat.

Charlie was pleased to see his master stepping into a butcher's shop. When he came out Scroat had a small packet tucked inside his coat.

Scroat's lodging was a tiny basement room in a tall house a few streets up from the river. Even on a cold night like this, the smell of raw sewage and dead fish wafting up from the river was disgusting. In summer, Charlie guessed, it would be even worse.

Scroat lit a small candle and a very small fire. Then he took from his jacket the package he had bought in the butcher's. Charlie's eyes looked up expectantly.

"What do you think I've bought then, boy? Pork chops or some tripe, perhaps?" he sneered, unwrapping a bottle from the paper. Easing off the cork he poured some of its contents onto a filthy rag. Charlie watched, fascinated.

Suddenly Scroat grabbed Charlie and started rubbing the rag on his elbows and knees.

"Yee–argh!" screeched Charlie. "That hurts." It was the first thing he had said all day.

"Stop yer racket, boy!" yelled Scroat. "It's only brine. The salt water they keep

fresh meat in. Yer knees and elbows need hardening up and rubbing this stuff in for a couple of weeks will do the trick."

Come early evening Scroat gave Charlie half a bowl of broth and bread.

"That's all you're getting. I know better than to feed up a climbing boy. The more boys eat, the bigger they get, and thin boys are best for climbing chimneys."

Still covered with soot from his day's work, Charlie curled himself up into a ball in the corner. Scroat threw a sack over him, then set off in the direction of the nearest public house.

Charlie's whole body ached. He heard a scurrying sound, and then felt a plop on the top of his sack. Opening his eyes he found himself staring into the watery pink eyes of a rat. It looked as hungry as Charlie himself.

He sat up painfully and the rat scampered away through a hole in the floor. "Oh, to be a rat," thought Charlie. And, at that moment, he just knew that somehow he had to escape from the clutches of Jeremiah Scroat.

Slowly, bit by bit, he retraced in his mind the events that had led him to the dreadful circumstances in which he found himself ...

## 2

## A Sudden Shock

The day before had started off pretty much like any other. Charlie and his mates, the Bromley brothers, were up to no good. They were on their way to visit a street of rich people's houses to play their favourite game – "Knock down Ginger".

This was, of course, Charlie's idea.

Proudly Charlie showed George and Billy Bromley a large bundle of string.

"Where d'yer get that?" George Bromley had asked.

"Friend of my Pa's," Charlie had replied.

Charlie's father had been a sailor and he had taught Charlie all kind of knots and hitches. His ship, *The Lady Gresham*, had been lost at sea the winter before last. As Charlie's mother had died shortly afterwards, he was being brought up by his elderly aunt.

Making sure nobody was around, Charlie skipped up the steps to the large front door and looped the end of the string round the door knocker. Then he tossed it over the brass lamp above the door and threaded it through the railings at the side of the steps. He carried on threading the string through the railings until he reached the end of the street. There he pulled the string. The knocker rattled with a satisfying thud-thud on the door. A maid came out with her face like thunder. Charlie, George and Billy couldn't contain their mirth. They all rolled round in one big, rollicking heap.

"Hey you there!"

Suddenly the boys saw the owner of the house, who had come out of the *back* door to catch them! They raced like the wind towards George and Billy's house.

"Charlie!" Liza, George and Billy's big sister, was at their front door. Normally she was a cheerful girl, but today her face was anxious.

"Charlie, you'd best get yourself home."

"Why?" Charlie felt a stab of panic in his stomach.

"Summat's happened." Liza grabbed him by the arms and gave

him a push in the direction of his home.

Charlie raced blindly along the streets until he reached his own house. Mrs Bromley, George and Billy's mother, stood in the hall.

"Oh Charlie Thompsett, what in the world's going to become of you?" she sobbed. "Your aunt, she's gone." Mrs Bromley shook her head sadly.

"Gone? Gone where?" Charlie's heart beat wildly.

"Heaven. I'm sure of that. She was an angel and a saint all rolled into one when she was living." She turned to Charlie. "Oh my poor lamb, whatever's going to become of you, now that all your relatives are dead?"

The undertaker came out of the house. "There's only one thing that can be done with him. He must be

handed over to the workhouse!"

As soon as Charlie heard the word 'workhouse', he turned on his heels and

ran. No one was putting Charlie Thompsett into the workhouse!

He ran until he was exhausted. Then he walked until the night began to close in. He realised he had no bed, no money, and no food. Food could of course be stolen, but the penalties for theft were severe – prison, transportation, or worse. Charlie found an alleyway, pulled

his thin jacket about him, and curled up
on the cobbles. He was cold and
uncomfortable, but more than that, he
was tired. He drifted off into a deep sleep.

"Bet you'd fancy a slice of bread and
dripping, eh boy?"

Charlie opened
his eyes. He found
himself looking up
into a grimy,
leathery face. The
face broke into a
terrifying grin,
revealing a row of
one yellow tooth
and two black
ones. Charlie was speechless.

"Orphan?"

Charlie nodded.

"This is your lucky day, boy!"

It didn't feel to Charlie
like a lucky day at all.

"You've got a
choice, boy," the
leathery-faced
man
continued.
"You can
throw
yourself on
the mercy of
the parish
workhouse, or
you can get
yourself
regular
food, shelter
and wages, by learning a
trade."

"What trade?" asked Charlie quickly.

"One of the most honourable trades in the country," replied the man. "The trade of Chimney Sweep. My name's Jeremiah Scroat. Chimney sweeping's my trade and I need a boy apprentice. What do you say?"

There was only one thing Charlie could say.

"Yes, sir. That is if you'll have me please, sir."

Charlie spent the night at Jeremiah Scroat's lodgings. He was given a slice of

bread and dripping for supper, and another slice for breakfast the next morning. Then he and Scroat set off for the Magistrate's house to get the papers signed which would make Charlie a legal apprentice. On the way back Scroat bought Charlie a sweep's cap with a brass badge. Scroat's name and address were engraved on the badge.

"Do you read, boy?" asked Scroat later as they sat in his lodgings.

"A little," said Charlie.

Scroat waved Charlie's apprenticeship papers – called indentures – in front of his face.

"It says here that you're bound to me as apprentice now for seven years."

Charlie nodded.

"It means that I own yer," growled Scroat. He put his face close to Charlie's. "I own yer," he repeated with an ugly sneer, "just as I might own a dog."

## 3

## Escape from Scroat

Now, one day into his career as an
apprentice sweep, Charlie lay shivering
and aching under his sack. He must have
drifted off to sleep, for the next thing he
knew he was being shaken awake roughly
by the arm.

"Get up, yer lazy bag o' bones!" roared Scroat. Soon Charlie was scrambling up the first chimney of the day. He could hardly bear the pressure on his grazed elbows and knees, but he pushed on. He had decided on a plan of escape.

As his sooty head popped out of the top of the chimney, he looked around him. The grey slates glistened with frost. Instead of inching himself back down the chimney, Charlie carried on pushing up. In no time at all he was on the roof. His knees hurt, but he didn't care. He was free. He started crawling faster, when suddenly a slate slipped and crashed to the ground. Charlie froze, but it was too late. The noise had alerted the household – and Scroat! Charlie climbed painfully down the drainpipe, not to freedom, but to a thrashing.

"Yer won't try that again in a hurry, will yer, my lad?" snarled Scroat.

"No, sir."

"Because you'd only get taken to the workhouse," said Scroat, smiling evilly at Charlie. "And yer better off with me, ain't yer?"

Slowly the days passed and winter turned to spring. The pain in Charlie's elbows and knees wore off, but not his fear of the tall, dark, narrow chimneys. That fear was getting worse. One morning he found himself so scared he just sat, wedged in the bottom of the chimney, unable to move.

"I'll get you up that chimney, yer lazy good-for-nothing," growled Scroat.

Charlie suddenly smelt smoke. He

heard the crackling of burning wood, and
then he felt a stab of pain as flames licked
the soles of his feet. Scroat had lit a fire!
He was "smoking" him up! Charlie let out
a scream of horror. He forgot his fear of
chimneys in his terror at being burned
alive. Up the chimney he went, choking in
the smoke, his feet toasted like tea cakes.

On their way home from work that day
Scroat stopped at a public house. Charlie

sat on the steps outside, hoping that his master would bring him something to eat.

Afternoon was darkening into evening when a rough hand yanked Charlie inside the pub. The air was thick with the smell of beer, tobacco and sweat. A gang of sailors were dancing, arms interlocked, singing lustily and out of tune. In the far corner sat Scroat, slumped over a table, drunk. Opposite him sat a younger sweep with a little pile of money in front of him. The man looked up at Charlie.

"So you're Scroat's apprentice?"

Charlie nodded.

"Not any more you ain't. He's just bet all his possessions on a game of cards with me, and he's lost. You're mine now. Come on!"

Scroat suddenly woke up from his drunken stupor. "You may have won the

boy – and a lazy, bone-idle boy he is – but you ain't won his clothes. I made no mention of what he was wearing. His clothes belong to me!"

Charlie backed off in horror as Scroat lunged at him, trying to rip his jacket off. Suddenly the younger man raised his fist and slammed it into Scroat's chin. In a flash Scroat was lying senseless on the floor. A cheer went up from the sailors as Charlie was pulled through the swaying crowd by his new master. "Come on, lad. I've got cold beef and pickles at home."

While they tucked into supper, Scroat's vanquisher introduced himself. "I'm 'Arry 'Awkins, sweep. That's 'Awkins with an

Haitch. No need to look at me like I'm going to eat you. I've always fancied having an apprentice. I was a climbing boy myself once, see."

★ ★ ★ ★

It was strange, but Charlie was never frightened of chimneys when he was with

Harry. Unlike Scroat, Harry didn't walk the streets looking for work, he had regular customers who booked him.

Then, a few months later, came the most terrifying day of Charlie's life. It began when they were standing outside a fine, large house.

"This is our first job today," said Harry. "Mr Parslow's new place. Ain't it grand? I used to do his old house, but this is my first time here."

"Mary will bring you a mug of tea," Mr Parslow said as Charlie began to take of his jacket. "It's hard and thirsty work you boys have to do."

Charlie liked what he saw of Mr Parslow, but he didn't like what he saw of his chimney. He poked his head round the screen.

"It ain't 'arf narrow," he said to Harry.

"Let's go up onto the roof," said Harry, "and we'll

see what it looks like from up there."

An icy wind was blowing across the rooftops.

"This looks wider," said Harry. "You'll be fine if you buff it."

"I ain't buffing it!" protested Charlie. "I ain't going stark naked down no chimney for no one." So Charlie took off his shirt, but kept his trousers on.

Down the chimney he went. As he edged down, he felt the sides of the chimney tightening on him. Then he

reached a kink in
the flue and found
that he couldn't
push himself
round the corner.

"Harry?"
Charlie's voice
was small with
terror and
foreboding.
"Harry, I'm
stuck!"

Scroat had
been right – big
boys don't make
good climbing
boys. And since he
had been working
with Harry,
Charlie had been

eating better and growing bigger by the
day.

"Push yourself back up!" shouted
Harry.

Charlie pushed, but found he hadn't
got the room to ease himself back up
either. Panicking, he tried
wriggling some more. The more he
struggled, the more he stuck fast.
Through his head flashed the tales
he had heard of climbing boys
suffocating to death in narrow
chimneys. He opened his
mouth to scream, but
found his mouth
was already filling
with soot.

Harry's
shouting had been
loud enough to be

heard throughout the house. Suddenly, Mr Parslow burst in.

"What's going on?"

"Boy's stuck," said Harry worriedly.

Mrs Parslow appeared and began to sob. "He won't die, Horace, will he? Not in our chimney?"

But Mr Parslow was already heading for the door. "I'll fetch a builder! We'll take the chimney down brick by brick if we have to!"

Charlie found himself drifting between

wakefulness and sleep. He did not know
how long he had been in the chimney
when he heard the thump, thump of
hammer and chisel on brick.

They lifted him out wheezing and

spluttering and laid him on the floor in the
Parslows' bedroom. After he'd coughed up
a stomachful of soot they gave him a cup
of beef tea to sip slowly. Mr and Mrs
Parslow wept with relief. Harry hugged

him. "I thought you were a gonner that time," he said. There were tears of joy in his eyes.

They swept no more chimneys that day.

"You've got too big for the climbing lark," said Harry. "And I'll tell you another thing. After what happened today, I don't feel like sending any more lads up

chimneys. The trouble is, what are you and I going to do for a living? Sweeping's the only trade I know."

It was a dismal supper for the two of them that evening. Cold mutton and gherkins had never seemed so dry before.

Suddenly, Harry and Charlie were startled out of their misery by a knock at the door.

"Mr Hawkins? My good sir, I'm glad I've found you!"

There on the doorstep stood Mr Parslow.

# 4

## A New Partnership

Mr Parslow declined Harry's offer of a
gherkin and a glass of ale.

"I'll come straight to the point," he
said. "Mrs Parslow and I were absolutely
terrified by what happened when you
swept our chimneys this morning."

"We were a mite anxious ourselves there for a bit, weren't we Charlie?" answered Harry.

"Yes," said Charlie, breaking out into a sweat just at the thought of it.

"So this afternoon, Mrs Parslow and I called on a friend of ours, a Mr Amos Catchpole. He is very active in the local branch of the Society for Superseding the Employment of Climbing Boys. Indeed, he is the inventor of Catchpole's Chimney

Cleansing Machine."

Harry raised a suspicious eyebrow.

"Mrs Parslow and I have joined their number. In short, we don't believe you should be sending boys up chimneys any more."

"Oh you don't, don't you?" Charlie noticed that Harry was getting rather red in the face.

"No," Mr Parslow continued. "And to that end, I am prepared to buy you one of Mr Catchpole's chimney cleansing machines."

Charlie's eyes lit up with excitement. He had heard talk of chimney sweeping machines, but had never seen one. It was Harry who spoke, though.

"I'm much obliged, I'm sure," he said, "but I don't take charity from any one." "But Harry – " protested Charlie.

"And I'll thank you to let me speak in my own house," replied Harry, sharply.

"Of course, if you wish, you could treat my offer as a loan and repay me the cost of the machine at such time as you are able," added Mr Parslow quickly.

Harry cocked his head this way and that. "Hmm … perhaps, yes … I would be pleased to accept your kind offer."

Next day, Harry and Charlie set off from Mr Parslow's with the new chimney cleansing machine. It consisted of a large round brush into which were screwed a series of flexible rods. Through the rods ran a long piece of string, so that if any of the rods broke off in the chimney, they wouldn't get lost.

Charlie pulled at the string. "Just like 'Knock down Ginger'," he laughed.

Harry looked thoughtful. "The way I see it is like this – these here rods are heavy. I ain't going to be able to manage them and carry a bag of soot. And another thing. If while I'm setting up the screen, I've got a mate screwing the rods together, and if while I'm unscrewing them, that mate bags up the soot, I'll get twice as much work done and twice as

much work means twice as much money!"

With a start Charlie saw Harry disappear into a printer's shop. Charlie followed him.

"I want a new trade card," Harry was saying to the printer. "It's for 'Awkins, with an Haitch ..." He turned and winked at Charlie. " – And Thompsett, Chimney Sweeps."

Hawkins and Thompsett
Chimney Sweeps

49 Nelson Street,
Portsea.

A broad beam spread across Charlie's face. "You and me? Partners?"

Harry grinned. "It's the least I can do," he said. "If you hadn't got stuck up Mr Parslow's chimney, he'd never have thought of buying us a machine, would he now? Come on. Don't stand there gawping. We'll go and buy a nice bit of tripe and onions for our supper. And some potatoes. You'll need feeding up if you're going to help me carry those great rods!"

# Notes

## Why climbing boys – and girls?

During the
late
eighteenth
and early
nineteenth
century,
coal became
a popular
household

fuel. Coal requires a good draught, and so
fireplaces and chimneys were made narrower.
These narrower chimneys became blocked with
soot. It was thought that the only thorough way of
cleaning these chimneys was to send children up
them with a brush. The first chimney sweeping
machine was invented as early as 1803, but most
people still preferred to use children.

## Pauper children

Many sweeps' boys were "parish children",
orphans who had been taken to the parish
workhouse. The "parish" – the town or village
council – could avoid having to pay for food and
keep for these orphans if they sold them to chimney
sweeps.

## Apprentices

Sweeps' boys were
apprentices. The local
magistrate signed
"indentures", legal
documents meant to
ensure that apprentices
were properly trained
and looked after by
their masters. In
practice, these
"indentures" were
often worthless.

## Injury and death

Being a climbing boy or girl was a dangerous occupation. Many children were killed after being suffocated or burnt in chimneys. Others fell off slippery  roofs. Endless hours spent in dark and narrow chimneys meant that climbing boys and girls often didn't grow properly. They might have damaged backs and knees. The rubbing of elbows and knees against the rough brickwork also gave them bad sores, and the soot damaged their eyesight.

## The climbing boy who survived

Despite terrible conditions some climbing boys and girls did survive. Peter Hall became a climbing boy at the age of six and a half, but he managed to live through all the hardships he experienced. When he grew up he travelled round the country checking up on master sweeps who were cruel to their apprentices. He took many of them to court, achieving no less than 400 convictions against them for breaking the law.

## The size of chimneys

If you want to imagine what it was like climbing a tall narrow chimney, cut out a piece of paper 23 centimetres square. That is the size of many of the chimneys children climbed. Then cut out a piece of paper 18 centimetres square. It is on record that a six-year-old girl climbed a chimney as narrow as this.

# Sparks: Historical Adventures

## ANCIENT GREECE
**The Great Horse of Troy** – The Trojan War
0 7496 3369 7 (hbk)   0 7496 3538 X (pbk)
**The Winner's Wreath** – Ancient Greek Olympics
0 7496 3368 9 (hbk)   0 7496 3555 X (pbk)

## INVADERS AND SETTLERS
**Boudicca Strikes Back** – The Romans in Britain
0 7496 3366 2 (hbk)   0 7496 3456 0 (pbk)
**Viking Raiders** – A Norse Attack
0 7496 3089 2 (hbk)   0 7496 3457 X (pbk)
**Erik's New Home** – A Viking Town
0 7496 3367 0 (hbk)   0 7496 3552 5 (pbk)
**TALES OF THE ROWDY ROMANS**
**The Great Necklace Hunt**
0 7496 2221 0 (hbk)   0 7496 2628 3 (pbk)
**The Lost Legionary**
0 7496 2222 9 (hbk)   0 7496 2629 1 (pbk)
**The Guard Dog Geese**
0 7496 2331 4 (hbk)   0 7496 2630 5 (pbk)
**A Runaway Donkey**
0 7496 2332 2 (hbk)   0 7496 2631 3 (pbk)

## TUDORS AND STUARTS
**Captain Drake's Orders** – The Armada
0 7496 2556 2 (hbk)   0 7496 3121 X (pbk)
**London's Burning** – The Great Fire of London
0 7496 2557 0 (hbk)   0 7496 3122 8 (pbk)
**Mystery at the Globe** – Shakespeare's Theatre
0 7496 3096 5 (hbk)   0 7496 3449 9 (pbk)
**Plague!** – A Tudor Epidemic
0 7496 3365 4 (hbk)   0 7496 3556 8 (pbk)
**Stranger in the Glen** – Rob Roy
0 7496 2586 4 (hbk)   0 7496 3123 6 (pbk)
**A Dream of Danger** – The Massacre of Glencoe
0 7496 2587 2 (hbk)   0 7496 3124 4 (pbk)
**A Queen's Promise** – Mary Queen of Scots
0 7496 2589 9 (hbk)   0 7496 3125 2 (pbk)
**Over the Sea to Skye** – Bonnie Prince Charlie
0 7496 2588 0 (hbk)   0 7496 3126 0 (pbk)
**TALES OF A TUDOR TEARAWAY**
**A Pig Called Henry**
0 7496 2204 4 (hbk)   0 7496 2625 9 (pbk)
**A Horse Called Deathblow**
0 7496 2205 9 (hbk)   0 7496 2624 0 (pbk)
**Dancing for Captain Drake**
0 7496 2234 2 (hbk)   0 7496 2626 7 (pbk)
**Birthdays are a Serious Business**
0 7496 2235 0 (hbk)   0 7496 2627 5 (pbk)

## VICTORIAN ERA
**The Runaway Slave** – The British Slave Trade
0 7496 3093 0 (hbk)   0 7496 3456 1 (pbk)
**The Sewer Sleuth** – Victorian Cholera
0 7496 2590 2 (hbk)   0 7496 3128 7 (pbk)
**Convict!** – Criminals Sent to Australia
0 7496 2591 0 (hbk)   0 7496 3129 5 (pbk)
**An Indian Adventure** – Victorian India
0 7496 3090 6 (hbk)   0 7496 3451 0 (pbk)
**Farewell to Ireland** – Emigration to America
0 7496 3094 9 (hbk)   0 7496 3448 0 (pbk)

**The Great Hunger** – Famine in Ireland
0 7496 3095 7 (hbk)   0 7496 3447 2 (pbk)
**Fire Down the Pit** – A Welsh Mining Disaster
0 7496 3091 4 (hbk)   0 7496 3450 2 (pbk)
**Tunnel Rescue** – The Great Western Railway
0 7496 3353 0 (hbk)   0 7496 3537 1 (pbk)
**Kidnap on the Canal** – Victorian Waterways
0 7496 3352 2 (hbk)   0 7496 3540 1 (pbk)
**Dr. Barnardo's Boys** – Victorian Charity
0 7496 3358 1 (hbk)   0 7496 3541 X (pbk)
**The Iron Ship** – Brunel's Great Britain
0 7496 3355 7 (hbk)   0 7496 3543 6 (pbk)
**Bodies for Sale** – Victorian Tomb-Robbers
0 7496 3364 6 (hbk)   0 7496 3539 8 (pbk)
**Penny Post Boy** – The Victorian Postal Service
0 7496 3362 X (hbk)   0 7496 3544 4 (pbk)
**The Canal Diggers** – The Manchester Ship Canal
0 7496 3356 5 (hbk)   0 7496 3545 2 (pbk)
**The Tay Bridge Tragedy** – A Victorian Disaster
0 7496 3354 9 (hbk)   0 7496 3547 9 (pbk)
**Stop, Thief!** – The Victorian Police
0 7496 3359 X (hbk)   0 7496 3548 7 (pbk)
**Miss Buss and Miss Beale** – Victorian Schools
0 7496 3360 3 (hbk)   0 7496 3549 5 (pbk)
**Chimney Charlie** – Victorian Chimney Sweeps
0 7496 3351 4 (hbk)   0 7496 3551 7 (pbk)
**Down the Drain** – Victorian Sewers
0 7496 3357 3 (hbk)   0 7496 3550 9 (pbk)
**The Ideal Home** – A Victorian New Town
0 7496 3361 1 (hbk)   0 7496 3553 3 (pbk)
**Stage Struck** – Victorian Music Hall
0 7496 3363 8 (hbk)   0 7496 3554 1 (pbk)
**TRAVELS OF A YOUNG VICTORIAN**
**The Golden Key**
0 7496 2360 8 (hbk)   0 7496 2632 1 (pbk)
**Poppy's Big Push**
0 7496 2361 6 (hbk)   0 7496 2633 X (pbk)
**Poppy's Secret**
0 7496 2374 8 (hbk)   0 7496 2634 8 (pbk)
**The Lost Treasure**
0 7496 2375 6 (hbk)   0 7496 2635 6 (pbk)

## 20th-CENTURY HISTORY
**Fight for the Vote** – The Suffragettes
0 7496 3092 2 (hbk)   0 7496 3452 9 (pbk)
**The Road to London** – The Jarrow March
0 7496 2609 7 (hbk)   0 7496 3132 5 (pbk)
**The Sandbag Secret** – The Blitz
0 7496 2608 9 (hbk)   0 7496 3133 3 (pbk)
**Sid's War** – Evacuation
0 7496 3209 7 (hbk)   0 7496 3445 6 (pbk)
**D-Day!** – Wartime Adventure
0 7496 3208 9 (hbk)   0 7496 3446 4 (pbk)
**The Prisoner** – A Prisoner of War
0 7496 3212 7 (hbk)   0 7496 3455 3 (pbk)
**Escape from Germany** – Wartime Refugees
0 7496 3211 9 (hbk)   0 7496 3454 5 (pbk)
**Flying Bombs** – Wartime Bomb Disposal
0 7496 3210 0 (hbk)   0 7496 3453 7 (pbk)
**12,000 Miles From Home** – Sent to Australia
0 7496 3370 0 (hbk)   0 7496 3542 8 (pbk)